CLIMATE CHANGE

WATER AND ICE

BY JIM OLLHOFF

VISIT US AT
WWW.ABDOPUBLISHING.COM

Published by ABDO Publishing Company, 8000 West 78th Street, Suite 310, Edina, MN 55439. Copyright ©2011 by Abdo Consulting Group, Inc. International copyrights reserved in all countries. No part of this book may be reproduced in any form without written permission from the publisher. ABDO & Daughters™ is a trademark and logo of ABDO Publishing Company.

Printed in the United States of America, North Mankato, Minnesota
052010
092010

 PRINTED ON RECYCLED PAPER

Editor: John Hamilton
Graphic Design: Sue Hamilton
Cover Photos: Thinkstock & iStockphoto
Interior Photo: AP-pgs 5, 8 & 23; Corbis-pgs 21, 26 & 27; Getty Images-pgs 12, 13, 20 & 29; iStockphoto-pgs 12, 16, 24 & 28; NASA-pgs 16 & 24 (Map-Robert Simmon); NOAA-pgs 22 & 25 (Map-Hugo Ahlenius UNEP/GRID-Arendal); Photo Researchers-pgs 9, 14 & 15; Thinkstock-pgs 1, 12 & 32; University of Colorado CIRES/Russell Huff & Konrad Steffen-pg 10; Visuals Unlimited-pgs 7, 11, 12 & 19.

Library of Congress Cataloging-in-Publication Data

Ollhoff, Jim.
   Water and ice / Jim Ollhoff.
      p. cm. -- (Climate change)
   Includes index.
   ISBN 978-1-61613-458-7
   1. Water--Juvenile literature. 2. Ice--Juvenile literature. I. Title.
   GB662.3.O59 2011
   551.46--dc22
                           2010005538

CONTENTS

WATER, WATER, EVERYWHERE

About three-fourths of the earth is covered in water. Oceans, glaciers, and ice caps are already the first casualty of climate change. Glaciers are melting, polar ice caps are thinning, and the acid levels of the oceans are increasing.

In the last century, ocean levels increased about 1.8mm (.07 inch) each year. In recent years, that amount has increased to more than 3 millimeters (.12 inch) per year. Since most of the world's population lives near coastlines, rising sea levels put the homes of millions of people at risk.

Humans pour about 22 million tons (20 million metric tons) of carbon dioxide into the atmosphere each day, mostly through the burning of fossil fuels. This greenhouse gas traps the sun's heat, changing the climate and changing the chemistry of the oceans.

Facing Page: Homes along the coast of Norfolk, England, are threatened by rising sea levels and erosion damage.

Scientists know that ice is melting and sea levels are rising. Scientists know that the oceans are becoming more acidic. However, the speed, amount, and effects of these changes are frustratingly uncertain.

HOW MUCH WILL SEA LEVELS RISE?

If climate change and global warming continue, how much will sea levels rise? Part of the answer depends on how warm the water will become. Water expands when it is warmer. The warmer it gets, the more sea levels will rise.

An even bigger cause of rising waters is melting ice. Within a few decades, the Arctic, around the North Pole, is expected to be ice-free in the summer months. However, when it melts, there will be only a small increase in ocean levels. This is because there is no land mass underneath the Arctic. It is simply frozen water. It's a little bit like a glass of water with ice cubes in it. When the ice cubes melt, the water level goes up only slightly, because most of the ice was under the surface of the water.

However, ice-covered Greenland and Antarctica are landmasses. If that ice melts, it will run into the ocean and cause a huge increase in sea levels. It's like piling up ice cubes on a flat plate. When the ice cubes melt, there is a big mess to clean up.

Facing Page: A huge chunk of Alaska's Surprise Glacier "calves off" (breaks away) into Prince William Sound. If too much glacial ice melts, the water will run into the oceans and cause flooding in coastal areas.

27th Session of the Intergovernmental on Climate Change

Above: The IPCC collects and reviews scientific climate studies and makes recommendations to world leaders.

The Intergovernmental Panel on Climate Change (IPCC) is a special research group created in 1988 by the United Nations. The IPCC collects and reviews scientific climate studies and makes recommendations to world leaders. In 2007, the IPCC estimated that the oceans would rise 7 to 23 inches (18 to 58 cm) by the year 2100. In 2009, new studies hint that ocean levels are rising even faster than these predictions.

Even a rise of a few inches will flood some island nations such as the Maldives or Tuvalu. Many residents of those nations have already had to relocate. Coastal villages in Alaska have had to relocate farther inland.

Predicting exactly how high ocean levels will rise is very difficult. There are many things scientists must account for in their calculations. For example, some studies assume that carbon dioxide levels in the atmosphere will remain the same. Other studies assume that carbon dioxide will increase, which will cause faster warming.

Because of these uncertainties, predictions vary a lot from study to study. Some scientists say ocean levels will rise 3 feet (.9 m) in the next 100 years. Others say the levels will rise 21 feet (6.4 m).

Even if ocean levels rise only 3 feet (.9 m), the effects will be very serious. Coastal cities will be overrun with water. Rich nations might be able to build massive—and expensive—levees to keep out the water. Many countries, such as Bangladesh and parts of Southeast Asia, will not be able to afford levees. Millions of people will have to move to higher ground.

The rise in ocean levels will not happen quickly. It will happen over a period of many decades. Still, even a small rise in sea levels will take a significant toll.

Left: If ocean levels rise only 3 feet (.9 m), coastal cities will be overrun with water. Rich countries may be able to build levees, or walls, to hold back the water, but poor nations could be devastated.

GREENLAND ICE

Greenland is the largest island in the world. About 80 percent of it is covered with ice. In fact, in many places the ice is 1.8 miles (2.9 km) thick. If all the ice on Greenland were to suddenly melt, the oceans would rise about 20 feet (6 m). That would flood most coastal cities of the world.

Luckily, Greenland ice won't melt suddenly. However, the giant glaciers and ice sheets in Greenland are indeed melting at an alarming rate. Greenland ice is melting twice as fast as it was just a decade ago.

Sea level rises aren't the same all over the world because of ocean currents and the curvature of the earth. Scientists predict that melting Greenland ice will have a much greater effect on the northeastern United States and eastern Canada.

Right: In 2005, scientists observed melting on huge portions of Greenland's ice sheet (area in peach). If this melting trend continues, sea levels may rise.

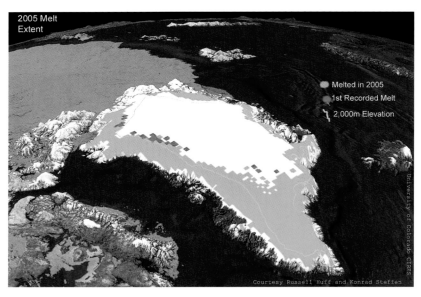

2005 Melt Extent

Melted in 2005
1st Recorded Melt
2,000m Elevation

University of Colorado CIRES

Courtesy Russell Huff and Konrad Steffen

A researcher looks at melted water on the Greenland ice sheet near Camp Victor, Ilulissat. The Greenland ice sheet is the largest ice sheet outside of Antarctica.

THE ARCTIC

Below: Loss of polar ice is a serious problem for the wildlife of the Arctic.

Harbor Seal

Narwhal

Polar Bear

Pacific Walrus

For thousands of years, the ice surrounding the North Pole had been stable. But in the late 19th century, people began pumping greenhouse gasses into the atmosphere. Today, average temperatures in the Arctic are rising twice as fast as they are in other parts of the globe.

The Arctic functions as a refrigerator for much of the world's climate. Changing the climate in the Arctic will have many effects. If one part of the world's climate is changed, there are ripple effects that happen all over the earth. For example, there might be more rain in the Mediterranean area during the winter, and more summer droughts in the southwest United States.

The loss of sea ice creates more waves. The more waves there are, the more erosion happens on the shoreline. On the north side of Alaska, between Prudhoe Bay and Barrow, 45 feet (14 m) of shoreline is lost every year. The rate that the land is lost has doubled in the last 25 years. This is an important habitat for wildlife. Loss of polar ice is especially a problem for seals, narwhals, polar bears, and Pacific walruses. Their habitats, migration patterns, and food sources are all affected. Some of these species might not even survive.

A home in Shishmaref, Alaska, has fallen victim to soil erosion.

ANTARCTICA

Antarctica is a landmass where the South Pole is located. It is mostly covered by giant sheets of ice. The ice of Antarctica holds much more water than Greenland's ice.

By drilling down into the Antarctic ice, it is possible for scientists to discover what the climate was like thousands of years ago. Researchers have discovered that during the last 14,000 years, there has been no warming like what is happening now.

Glaciers and ice sheets are retreating all over the continent. Up until the year 2000, the eastern ice sheet seemed stable. This led some non-scientists to conclude that global warming wasn't really happening. But what was actually occurring was that the weather had changed over Antarctica because of the man-made hole in the ozone layer. Winds increased, which caused melting on the western side of the continent, but much less melting on the eastern side.

Since 2002, scientists have measured significant thinning and loss of the eastern ice sheet. Antarctica loses about 220 billion tons (200 billion metric tons) of ice per year. Ninety percent of Antarctic glaciers have retreated.

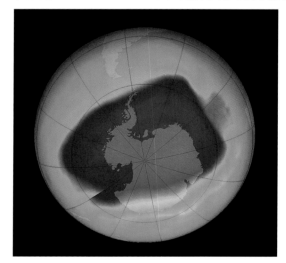

A scientist drills down to get an ice core sample in Antarctica. By studying this ice, researchers can discover what the climate was like thousands of years ago.

GLACIERS

A glacier is like a huge frozen river. It's a giant mass of ice that flows, ever so slowly, from high mountain areas to lower areas, sometimes to the ocean. When it snows, glaciers grow. When the weather is warm, glaciers melt, or retreat.

In summers, when glaciers melt, they often provide drinking water for people. In fact, about 75 percent of the world's people rely on glaciers for drinking water. Glacial meltwater provides water for rivers and replenishes underground water, called aquifers.

In the past 50 years, glaciers all over the world have been melting far more than usual. Winters are shorter and warmer, so glaciers don't get a chance to refreeze and regrow to their normal size.

Below: Grey Glacier in Chile's Torres del Paine National Park, as seen from the International Space Station. This huge frozen river of ice flows from the Patagonian Andes Mountains into Grey Lake.

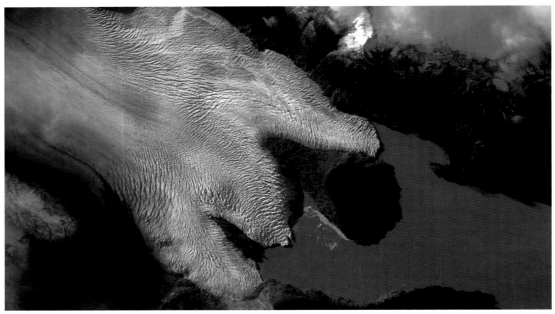

A man skis near a glacier in Antarctica.

Most glaciers across the world are melting, but not every single one. Sometimes changes in local weather patterns allow isolated glaciers to grow.

Glaciers melt faster when they melt at the top and bottom at the same time. The summer sun heats the top of the glacier, forming a lake of water on top. The warm water burrows down, melting ice below it. This river of melted ice water flows through a chute called a moulin, which can reach all the way down to the bottom of the glacier. The glacier then develops a layer of warmer water on the bottom as well as the top. This makes it easier for the glaciers to move faster, sometimes sliding off into the ocean. This process of melting at the top and bottom is often difficult to detect. It makes many scientists worry that glaciers will melt faster than predicted.

A miner holds a canary.

In the 1800s and earlier, when miners went deep underground, they would bring a canary or other small birds with them. The miners needed a way to know when the oxygen was about to run out. They knew that if the canary died, then oxygen was low, and they had to get out quickly. Since then, any predictor of something ominous is called "a canary in a coal mine." Climatologists refer to glaciers as "the canary in climate change's coal mine." Glaciers are one of the first things affected by climate change, and they predict bigger changes in the future.

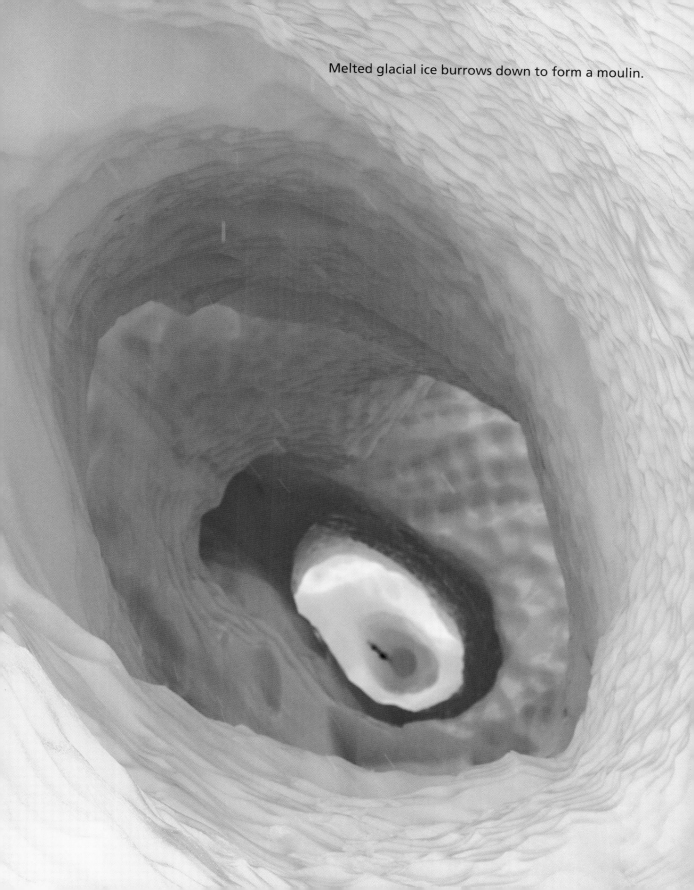

Melted glacial ice burrows down to form a moulin.

OCEANS

Climate change affects the earth's oceans in many ways. Two problems that worry climatologists and marine biologists the most are increases in ocean temperature and increases in ocean acidity.

Ocean acidity is sometimes called the "other carbon problem." Carbon dioxide traps the sun's heat in the earth's atmosphere. It also chemically reacts with seawater to increase the amount of acid in the water. Most animals in the ocean can only survive in a very narrow range of ocean acidity. If the water becomes too acidic, it threatens the wide diversity of life in the oceans. Water measured along the California shoreline is already acidic enough, at times, to be dangerous to shellfish.

Below: Increasing ocean acidity is making it difficult for tiny pteropods to form shells.

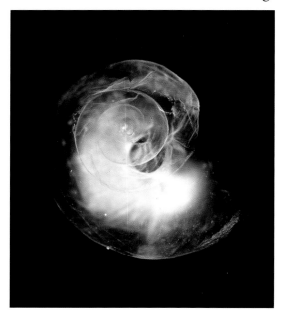

Small creatures are the most vulnerable to ocean acidity. For example, there are some species of tiny creatures, called pteropods, that have very thin shells. As ocean water becomes more acidic, pteropods have difficulty making shells. Pteropods are extremely important in the food web. They are food for fish. If one part of the food web disappears, it will have consequences for all forms of life in the ocean.

Above: Commercial fishermen and other boaters form the words "acid ocean" during an event held to spread the message of saving the oceans from high acid levels caused by fossil fuel emissions. More than 100 boats and hundreds of members of the fishing community took part in the September 2009 event in Homer, Alaska.

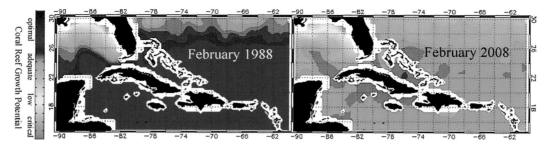

optimal adequate low critical

Coral Reef Growth Potential

February 1988

February 2008

Above: A graph showing the decrease in coral reef growth potential from 1988 to 2008 in the Gulf of Mexico, the Caribbean Sea, and portions of the Atlantic Ocean.

Since the start of the Industrial Revolution, when people started burning fossil fuels, ocean acidity has increased about 30 percent. At current rates, ocean acidity may double by the end of the century.

Coral reefs are stony structures on the ocean floor that are created by living organisms. Almost one-quarter of all ocean species live in or near coral reefs. They are a center of life and activity. But coral reefs are very sensitive. Increasing water temperature and increasing acidity have hit coral reefs hard. Many coral reefs have died or greatly reduced in size over the past 20 years. The loss of diversity affects the food web in the ocean. There is some hope that coral reefs will become more tolerant of changing waters. But long-term survival is doubtful if climate-related threats are not reduced.

The oceans and the diversity of life they contain have always absorbed excess carbon dioxide from the earth's atmosphere. However, the oceans may have reached their limit of carbon dioxide absorption. Experiments conducted by climatologists have shown worrisome results. Some show that the oceans can no longer absorb any more carbon dioxide. Other experiments say they can absorb a little more. Either way, humanity's continued burning of fossil fuels has overtaken the oceans' ability to capture and absorb carbon dioxide.

Above: Researchers with the National Oceanic and Atmospheric Administration (NOAA) study a coral reef near Key West, Florida. People are concerned that coral reefs are dying, largely because of climate change, overfishing, and pollution.

WORST-CASE SCENARIO

A climate change effect that some scientists fear most is a shutdown of the North Atlantic current. Here's how the North Atlantic current normally works: The ocean currents act like a conveyer belt, bringing warm water from the equator northward. The current eventually flows near the coast of northern Europe. Thanks in part to the North Atlantic current, areas such as the United Kingdom, Ireland, and Scandinavia have moderate, livable climates, even though they are in northern latitudes.

As the warm water moves into the North Atlantic, it cools down and becomes saltier because of evaporation. (Pure water goes into the air, leaving behind much of the salt.) Salty, cold water sinks. The current then returns through deep water to the equator, where it eventually warms and moves to the surface again. Then it begins its journey back to the North Atlantic. This giant conveyer belt is called the thermohaline circulation.

Below: The Gulf Stream brings warm water from the equator northward, causing northern areas such as Ireland to have a warmer, more livable climate.

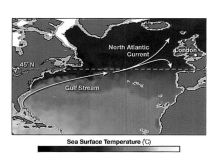

Sea Surface Temperature (°C)

-2   35

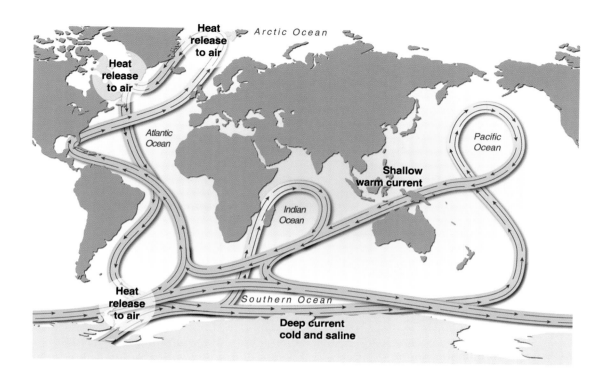

Because of global warming, glaciers in Greenland and the Arctic are melting at an alarming rate. Massive amounts of fresh water are being poured into the salty ocean. Some scientists fear that the fresh water will overwhelm the natural thermohaline circulation, and the cold, salty water will no longer sink. This would mean that the thermohaline system of circulation shuts down. The problem is that northern Europe draws its seasonally warm climate from this tropical current. If the thermohaline circulation shuts down, then the temperatures of Europe could drop about 20 degrees Fahrenheit (about 11 degrees C) or more. Plunging temperatures could jeopardize millions of lives and devastate the European economy.

Above: Cool, salty water travels from the North Atlantic to the equator, where it warms up and moves to the surface. The warm water then travels back northward. This giant conveyer belt is called the thermohaline circulation.

Above: A snow-covered forest. Cold temperatures could be in store for northern Europe if global warming causes a change in the ocean's thermohaline circulation.

It seems strange that one of the effects of global warming might be plunging temperatures in northern Europe. But that's exactly what some scientists fear. They have compared today's ocean circulation with measurements taken in the 1960s. They found that the speed of the thermohaline circulation has slowed by about 30 percent.

Worse yet, climatologists know this thermohaline circulation has shut down before. About 12,000 years ago, there was a massive lake in North America called Lake Agassiz. It held more water than all of today's Great Lakes combined. For some reason, natural earthen dams broke away, and a huge amount of fresh water emptied into the North Atlantic. This flood of fresh water shut down the thermohaline circulation system in a matter of a few months. Northern Europe plunged into an ice age for hundreds of years.

Scientists still don't agree if or when a thermohaline circulation shutdown would happen, or whether the shutdown would be slow or fast. Much depends on how world leaders take action to limit the effects of global warming.

Above: If a thermohaline circulation shutdown would happen, it's unknown whether the climate changes would be fast or slow.

STOPPING THE MELT

Given enough time, nature can heal itself. Oceans can reduce their acidity, glaciers can grow again. Greenland, Antarctica, and the Arctic can expand their ice. Ocean levels can be reduced. The rich diversity of plants and animals on land and in the oceans can return.

The earth can repair itself over time, but only if people stop adding to the damage. The solution is not an easy one. Most climatologists agree that we must find a way to stop burning fossil fuels to generate electricity. Burning fossil fuels pours too much carbon dioxide into the earth's atmosphere. This increases the greenhouse effect, which warms the earth too much. Maybe wind, solar, and nuclear power can help us kick the habit of burning fossil fuels. But whatever solution we choose, the world's governments and industries must put the plan into action quickly.

We have the knowledge and tools to solve global warming today. Do we have the determination to use them?

Facing Page: Given time, nature can heal itself, bringing back the beauty of the world.

Below: If we are to stop the damage, we need to stop burning fossil fuels.

28

GLOSSARY

CARBON DIOXIDE

Normally a gas, carbon dioxide is a chemical compound made of two oxygen atoms and one carbon atom. Its chemical symbol is CO_2. It is created by burning fossil fuels. It is the leading cause of the greenhouse effect and global warming.

FOSSIL FUEL

Fuels that are created from the remains of ancient plants and animals that were buried and then subjected to millions of years of heat, pressure, and bacteria. Oil and coal are the most common fossil fuels burned to create electricity. Natural gas is also a fossil fuel. Burning fossil fuels releases carbon dioxide into the atmosphere, contributing to global warming.

GLACIER

An immense sheet of ice that moves over land, growing and shrinking as the climate changes. Glaciers carve and shape the land beneath them. Glaciers today are found in the polar regions, and in mountainous areas. They hold vast reserves of fresh water.

GREENHOUSE EFFECT

Just as heat is trapped in a greenhouse by glass, certain gasses in the atmosphere trap the sun's heat and warm the earth. The surface of the earth absorbs some solar radiation, and reflects some. The reflected rays either pass back into space, or are absorbed and reflected back by gasses in the earth's atmosphere. Carbon dioxide is a major greenhouse gas that is produced by burning fossil fuels. When too much solar radiation is absorbed, the earth warms up, which alters climates around the world.

Greenhouse Gas

Any gas that is good at absorbing and retaining the sun's heat. Carbon dioxide, which is released into the atmosphere by the burning of fossil fuels, is a greenhouse gas. Greenhouse gasses contribute to a gradual warming of the earth, which is called the greenhouse effect.

Industrial Revolution

A time in the 1800s and 1900s when huge scientific advances were made in machine technology. The world's economies started relying more on manufacturing instead of farming and manual labor.

IPCC (Intergovernmental Panel on Climate Change)

An organization set up by the United Nations. The IPCC's job is to advise governments on the issue of climate change.

Moulin

A tubular chute through which melted glacial ice water burrows down to the ground at the bottom of the glacier.

Ozone Layer

An upper layer of the atmosphere containing high levels of ozone. Ozone is a gas that absorbs the sun's damaging ultraviolet radiation.

Thermohaline Circulation

The ocean currents that bring tropical warm water (and thus warmer temperatures) to northern Europe.

United Nations

Formed in 1945, an organization of representatives from 192 nations with the mission of promoting peace, security, and economic development on a worldwide basis.

INDEX